MAGNIFICENT JOURNEY

by Wm. Edwin Jacobs

Victory Publishing Company

Decatur, Illinois

MAGNIFICENT JOURNEY

Published by Victory Publishing Co.,
First Printing, January 2008

For information or to purchase additional copies contact:
Victory Publishing Company
3797 North Ashley Court
Decatur, IL 62526-1291

Telephone: (217) 872-7401.   e-mail: edmar84@aol.com

(Cost: $8.00 per copy, plus $2.00 mailing within the U.S.A.)

ISBN: 978-0-9778925-1-8

To

My daughter Vickie,
my miracle from God,
always and forever.

There is a land of the living and a land of the dead and the bridge is love, the only survival, the only meaning.

from
<u>The Bridge of San Luis Rey</u>
by, Thornton Wilder

PREFACE

Many thanks to my wife, Maria, who frequently suggested that I publish this story. In the work involved in bringing that to fruition, she has remained my faithful helpmate, as in every aspect of my life.

All quotations from the Bible are from the NIV unless otherwise indicated.

A hand touched me and set me trembling on my hands and knees. He said, "Daniel, you who are highly esteemed, consider carefully the words I am about to speak to you, and stand up, for I have now been sent to you." And when he said this to me, I stood up trembling.

Then he continued, "Do not be afraid, Daniel. Since the first day that you set your mind to gain understanding and to humble yourself before your God, your words were heard, and I have come in response to them."

Daniel 10:10-12

CONTENTS

INTRODUCTION

All of the events in both the major and minor narratives actually happened; none of it is fiction. However, the theology that is interspersed in the narrative naturally runs the risk of being regarded as pure invention. Nevertheless, the events of the main narrative, to the best of my remembrance, are the events that actually took place on that New Year's Eve. Some of the exact details regarding minor turns in the trail are a little hazy at this point in time, and therefore at minor points they may not accurately reflect the topology of the ridge. But I do distinctly remember the feelings, sensations, and thoughts of that evening, and I need only close my eyes to remember again the images and feelings which became indelibly etched in my memory.

There is an Oriental belief that life is divided into three phases. The first one is from birth to about twenty years of age; it is the period of growing up and of schooling. Second is the approximately twenty year period of work and family. The third period of twenty years, or however long life on earth lasts, is spent integrating life, bringing some sense of unity and purpose to life. Some people get lost in the memories, and there usually are many precious memories that we carry with us – the burden is light. It is the sorrows and failures and sins that weigh us down. We need to drop them at the foot of the cross of Christ before we can make any real "Pilgrim's Progress" toward the City of God.

I remember Professor John Killinger commenting in a seminary class that many of the cases of so-called dementia, are not a physical disability, but rather a being totally engrossed in memories, trying to make some sense and unity out of the multitude of events that make up their personal history. Their attention needs to be drawn to the events of the present, and a balance achieved. As Viktor Frankl noted, "The past is the treasure house of accomplishments, and the present is the opportunity to redeem the mistakes of the past." It is a call to action as well as reflection. And we all have numerous reasons for needing redemption before we are called to present ourselves before his Excellency, the Lord Christ who rules and judges in behalf of God the Father Almighty.

The Journey herein recorded was a happy event imprinted in my memory, remarkable for the extraordinary intensity of my aliveness to life in that present moment. It was a time of total focus, and consequently of a sense of the presence of God, in whom we live and move and have our being.

ONE

It is an odd kind of trail, I thought as I started up it. Steps had been cut into the side of the mountain ridge, but now they were nearly filled in with snow packed down to a slippery firmness by what appeared to have been the foot-steps of many people who had climbed the trail since the snow had fallen.

I turn and wave to Maria who is standing on the walk way near the corner of the lodge in the graying light of early evening. She returns my wave, and then turns toward the lodge walking slowly and thoughtfully. She had not wanted to climb the ridge this evening, so soon after we had arrived at the lodge. But I was intent on it.

The clerk at the desk had said the snow would be gone by morning because rain is expected tonight, and I wanted to see the snow-covered mountains from the top of the ridge; that was the whole point of coming to the lodge this New Year's Eve in the mountains of East Kentucky – to see the snow-covered mountains. The view from the top should be majestic. They are beautiful from a distance and close up.

As I turn and resume my climb it seems like I am entering a winter wonderland. The trail is like a tunnel of green and white. There is a scrub type of tree whose leaves are thick, broad, and shiny green like a magnolia tree leaf. The strange thing is that the trees have not shed these leaves during this brisk mountain winter. Perhaps they are a stunted type of magnolia tree. The snow is stacked up on the leaves, and under the weight of it they completely over-hang the trail and form a sparkling tunnel of green and white – it stretches onward and upward as far as I can see, which isn't much over a quarter of a mile due to a bend in the trail.

I need to hurry, because the time concerns me. What a pity not to be able to leisurely take my time and absorb the striking beauty of this scene. I've never seen anything like it before. But I need to hurry; before beginning the climb up the trail my calculations had been based on my being able to maintain an average three miles per hour. In a brisk walk a person can do that; the trail had not appeared too steep, and I was gambling that I could beat sundown by averaging three miles per hour on both the climb and descent.

On this trail it is a half of a mile to the top of the natural bridge, and a mile down on the other trail. That means a half hour trip in theory, and there was forty-five minutes to one hour till sundown when I started. Even if my estimated speed erred too much, even by a factor of two, I should reach the lodge right about at sundown. Under no circumstances do I want to spend the night alone and without shelter on the mountain. I have got to be off the mountain come sundown.

It is refreshing now to hurry up the trail, sometimes taking two steps in a stride; it was a long fatiguing drive from Shakertown, driving in blowing snow, and on snow-covered roads half of the way here. This climb is just what I need to stretch my legs, and my whole body – for sometimes the trail is so steep that I can touch it in front of me with my hands as I lean into the climb. The beauty of the snow-covered mountain side, with every leaf and limb and twig stacked with snow, reminds me of my youthful days in Indiana. It seemed like every winter there was at least one time when sleet fell, and froze as it hit, causing ice to form around everything and icicles to hang from everything – every wire, every twig and limb; it also caused a sheet of ice to form on the ground, and nobody, except me, seemed to like that.

Invariably, the sleet would turn to snow, and then there would be several inches of snow stacked up on top of everything encased with ice, with the icicles hanging below. It turned the most mundane places into a work of art – nature's way of tinkering with scenery, and providing a little variety. But then, every season was a delight to me, and a thing of beauty.

Nature has always been sacred to me, God's creation, and from the beauty of it, and the panorama of change, it is no wonder that God pronounced it "good, good" when he looked upon what he had made. [There was no Hebrew word then for "very."]

The only ugliness that has come into it is where mankind has touched it and changed it. But that ability to change and modify the physical environment of the world as we know it comes as a two-edged gift; after all some of the buildings and lawns and gardens are beautiful in their own right, and even occasionally they are a work of art – and in that sense, mankind creates (really just fashions), and perhaps that is one of the things that Jesus was referring to when,

Jesus answered them [his critics], "Is it not written

in your Law, 'I have said you are gods'? If he called
them 'gods,' to whom the word of God came [Psalm
82:6] – and the Scripture cannot be broken – what
about the one whom the Father set apart as his very
own and sent into the world?"

(John 10:34-36a)

I remember how my love of nature used to get me
into a little trouble as a kid. In my pre-teen and early teen
years it was my turn to mow the lawn at home with the push-
type mower. Usually I had to be told several times to do it,
not because I was lazy, but because I preferred to see grass
grow to its natural height so it could wave in the breeze. It
seemed like such a desecration to clip it off before it reached
its natural height. Nobody seemed to see it my way, consequently my mother always prevailed. I performed the sacri-
ficial rite, all in the name of civilization.

This is a pragmatic age, and philosophy gives way to
uniformity. But my reverence for life, even plant life, is not
unique to me, nor did Albert Schweitzer originate it; but he
did popularize it.

It was the prophet Isaiah who said of the coming
Messiah, "A bruised reed he will not break." (Isaiah 42:3a)
This relationship to nature dates back thousands of years,
and I like to think that the prophecy was literally true – that
"gentle Jesus" of the childhood prayer, is just that gentle,
that he has regard for all life. The one through whom the
world was created, came and walked among his people and
had regard for all life, even a reed. It is in keeping with the
accounts of his life recorded in the New Testament.

Even his cursing of the fig tree does not conflict with

that, for there is a certain rigid justice to nature – and you violate its laws at your own peril. Note that the tree had leaves, but no figs. I know from experience that if it had leaves, there should have been figs. There was a hypocrisy in its appearance.

It seems like everybody thinks St. Paul was speaking metaphorically of consciousness as a characteristic of all creation in regards to the curse that God put on the ground as a consequence of the fall of Adam and Eve, recorded in the Genesis account. But I like to think that he was not speaking metaphorically, but that all of creation is bound up in the future of the church, that the dignity of the faith is just that grand. And that when the Church Militant (alive on earth today) together with the Church at Rest (those in heaven) become the Church Victorious, by the grace of God, then nature too shall find its rest, exempt from the kill and be killed law of the forest that now gives a starkness to it, and that then the lion and the lamb shall lie down together when the rebellion of mankind ceases, when "time" is called on human history.

TWO

My right boot slips on the wet packed snow, and I go sprawling forward, catching myself with my hands. As I lie here for a moment, the snow feels pleasantly cool against my right cheek. I'm only a little over-heated and winded, and the deep breaths come easily. Then it dawns on me that the air I'm breathing is really not very cold, and there is hardly any breeze stirring.

In the quiet of the forest there is only one sound that I hear now. It is the occasional dripping of the trees. The temperature must be just barely above 32 degrees; that accounts for the slightly wet surface of the snow. As slippery as that is I'm going to have to pay more attention to what I'm doing, rather than getting lost in thought. A broken leg or arm now could be disastrous.

As I stand up I can see there are only a few more steps cut into the side of the ridge, then the trail is smooth as it slopes up moderately. Passing the last of the steps I find I'm out of the tunnel of leaves and snow; the trees are much taller here and spaced farther apart. The trail meanders, making abrupt turns in switch-backs, but it is easier now – walking briskly rather than climbing. It occurs to me that something has changed; alarmingly I realize that the light is dimmer. The change has occurred so subtly that I failed to notice it as it was happening; the sky is heavily overcast, perhaps that is why. The question is "Should I go on?" I seem to be near the top, and it would be a shame to have to turn around now and retrace my steps.

The scenery would be different down the other trail, yet it is a longer trail – twice as long. But it would be down-hill and quicker going. The view from the top, with the snow on the mountains, should be so beautiful that it would be a pity to miss it after coming this close, and besides, the snow will probably be gone in the morning.

That decides it; I'll go on to the top. It's risky, but I trust nature. Being here in the snow-covered woods feels like being at home – a sense of elation – after the years spent in the heat of Florida with only occasional respites. Besides, the trip down will go quickly.

I remember my trip down Mt. Fujiyama in Japan. That was one of the most dangerous and craziest things I ever did. The trip up was not particularly dangerous, in fact, hardly at all, just fatiguing. I was in the Air Force then, stationed at the 548th Reconnaissance Squadron at Yokota Air Force Base, about thirty miles NNW of Tokyo; formerly it was a Kamikaze base during World War II. There were a half a dozen of us from my squadron that decided to climb Mt. Fuji.

I was twenty years old then, with all the confidence of youth, and as we stood on the top of the mountain that Saturday morning in the swirling mists of the wind driven cloud, we decided to take the quick way down because we wanted to be back at the base that night.

There was an ash slide down one side of the mountain, only about a mile from the trail up; it ran parallel to the trail and ended not far from the beginning of the trail. It had an angle of declination of about 40 degrees to 50 degrees, and from my background in geometry and trigonometry I would have sworn that it was closer to 50 degrees. On the way up we had seen the slide and where it dished out to an end at the timberline near the trail.

As we looked at the slide from the top end of it, it was made up of that charcoal colored, cinder-like volcanic ash that was mainly the size of a coarse grade of sand, with chunks that varied in size all the way up to boulders a yard in diameter. As we debated on whether or not to try to go down it, we wondered how deep we would sink into it – up to our knees or waist? We decided to try it, and if it didn't work out we would hike over to the trail which lay to the right of us.

As we started down, we found that we sank into the ash up to our ankles. Needless to say, we were glad that we had worn our combat boots. The curious thing was that by standing upright in the ash, I could turn half way around and touch it behind me without bending over; it was just that steep.

I was a little bit apprehensive about starting an avalanche. But the view was breath-taking, and not just because of the 12,400 feet altitude; the slide seemed to slope away beneath us at a dizzying angle, and it stretched for several miles before meeting the timberline. It was one of the most astonishing situations I have ever been in.

We started down slowly at first, but as we realized that we were not going to sink into the ash above our ankles, and that we needed to speed up if we were going to stick to our time-table, we got a little braver. It was exhilarating to take a step out into space and drop about six to eight feet before my boot started digging into the ash again, and I would slide several feet — digging a furrow before stopping. But before I came to a complete stop I would stride out into space again and the sequence would repeat, only faster. Because of gravity the tempo kept speeding up, and the ash around me started to slide as it got entrained in the frenzy of motion. I was half sure that I could beat any avalanche I started. But as I went faster and faster, no matter how much I lay back against the ash as I would dig my feet in to slow the descent, my balance still tended to shift forward. To wind up going head over heels down that ash slide would cut a person to ribbons. So when things felt like they were beginning to get out of control, I took the climbing stick that I had been holding cross-wise in front of me, and used it under my right arm and held it against my side as I lay all the way back against the ash and dug both of my heels in. It took what seemed like a dozen feet or more in distance to stop, and by that time I was laughing with sheer delight at the pure adventure of it.

To go up against nature, and lay my life on the line, and survive and win by strength and agility was a fascinating and exhilarating thing to do. A you-bet-your-life proposition; and to win in it gave a sense of power and, strangely enough, of peace. The occasional utter dangerousness of nature was challenging; I wouldn't have it any other way.

At the time I was quite aware of the danger the ash presented. Sometimes there would be a large volcanic rock just barely covered by the finer grained ash, and when my foot started to dig into the ash and hit one of those rocks, it was absolutely essential that my ankle be straight and my knee slightly bent. To stumble or to sprain an ankle in such a fast moving dangerous situation was almost certain to end in injury if not in death. But then, by definition, life is made for living. And I knew my physical capabilities, and their limits, and proceeded accordingly, and even went to the full extent now and then.

On the occasions when I stopped, the view was fantastic. I could see across the smaller mountains surrounding Mt. Fuji, and when I looked East, I could see Tokyo and Yokohama on the horizon.

We made it to the timberline in record time, or at least I did; I was leading the pack, and we were strung out for nearly half of a mile down that slope. It was great fun. The experience was then behind me, and any return would be a rerun. I knew the secrets of the mountain – or at least, as much as I wished to know – the tinkling temple bells in the swirling mists on the rim of the crater, and the black-robed holy men asking for alms. It was like a different world there at the top; the Torii – the Shinto gateway consisting of two uprights supporting a curved lintel with a straight cross-piece below it – at the top of the trail was our entry into a world strangely different from anything I had ever seen before.

After the trip up the mountain, as before, on a clear day I could see Mt. Fuji from Yokota Air Force Base, rising majestically from the horizon in the south west. It was a frequent reminder of the thrill of my journey. But I never went back to the mountain again. There was a saying in Japan that he who comes to Japan and does not climb Mt. Fujiyama is a fool, and he who climbs it twice is a fool. I think it is true.

THREE

The light is very dim now, and I'm worried about sundown. Not by the wildest stretch of my wild imagination do I want to spend the night on this mountain without a tent and heater. It would be sheer madness to want to do it; and I certainly don't want to.

It's difficult to see the trail now – it's white against white, and in this deepening darkness it is getting harder to distinguish the trail. As I grab onto an oak tree to pull myself up past a particularly steep and slippery part of the trail, I come to what seems like a dead end. "It can't be!"

Kneeling down in the dim light I can just barely make out that the trail branches here. One branch goes off to the left between some trees and the other branch goes to the right. The right hand branch looks a little clearer, besides, it's the one I need to take because the trail down lies to the right of the one I'm on.

What is worrisome is that in this gathering darkness, since I'm having difficulty seeing the trail, it would be very easy to wander off it and be lost in this snow covered forest on the mountain. There is the added danger of the temperature going lower, or of falling off of a drop-off and being injured to where I can't move and then slowly freezing to death.

I'm aware of those dangers and it worries me a little, but not all that much. And there is no panic. "I wonder why?" But I've always felt at home in the woods, at least that was the case in Indiana. Nature has always seemed to me a friend and not an enemy.

I guess it goes all the way back to my earliest child-hood. I was raised in the church, and I can still remember one hymn we use to sing,

> This is my Father's world,
> And to my list'ning ears,
> All nature sings,
> And round me rings,
> The music of the spheres.
> This is my Father's world,
> I rest me in the thought
> Of rocks and trees,
> Of skies and seas,
> His hand the wonders wrought.

It has never occurred to me to doubt that the world and myself were created by God, so that there is a funda-mental unity. At least there is a fundamental for-ness rather than an against-ness.

My earliest remembrance as a child is from my pre-school years. I was in a vacant lot across the street from my home. The neighbors had cut down a tree there, and several of the branches were positioned just right, so that I could lie back on them with my feet barely touching the ground. I could rock the branches of the tree as I lay there looking up at the blue sky with the brilliantly white fluffy clouds float-ing by on that spring day. I can still remember that supreme sense of contentment that I had then – watching the clouds go by. I didn't move for the longest time, just gently rocking and watching the clouds go by, at peace with God and all of the world, even that marvelously intricate fallen tree. Life was just the way it ought to be, I thought then, and I guess it was. What a pity that all of the years since then have not brought me the serenity that I knew then. But, looking backwards, perhaps the lesson to be learned is that it was I who stopped all other activities and climbed onto the limbs to take a look at the creation in operation.

In many of the activities of life since then there has not seemed to be a getting off place, no time to become at peace with myself and the world. That was one of the reasons for coming to this mountain this New Year's Eve, to find a getting-off place, and a time to wonder, and a time to decide. Maybe that's what New Year's Eves are for.

FOUR

The trail is flattening out now, and the walking is not as hard as it was. There's hardly any noise to my walking in the snow. "Something is wrong! There's not enough noise. There's a noise missing." I stop and listen, but there is no sound except an occasional creak from a tree limb flexing under the weight of the snow in the barely perceptible breeze. Then I realize the noise that is missing.

The trees have stopped dripping, and that means that the temperature has fallen below 32° F. This is serious. Maybe the warmer air mass and the rain will not get here by morning. That could mean more snow tonight, and probably a temperature in the mid-twenties.

It's darker now. Of course, I'm in the shade of the trees, but I will also be in the shade going down the other trail, and it will be darker then. This situation is becoming more dangerous the farther I go. That's a curious thing about nature; it is almost indifferent to the existence of mankind. A fall off of a cliff will kill a person as easily as it will an animal. Lightening will kill a person as easily as most other creatures. I guess if you ranked the universe on a scale of positive to negative, according to whether the universe was for or against mankind, it would have to be ranked as zero positive. For although nature seems to be almost indifferent to mankind, there is a deference given by nearly every creature on earth. There are only a few fish in the ocean that will initiate an attack on a person, and on the North American continent there are only two of the species of bears that will start an attack. It seems that all of the rest of the animals, except the buffalo which is not found except in preserves and farms, will only fight a person if cornered. As it stands, there is just enough danger in the forest to make it interesting. It almost seems like the God given dominance of mankind is acknowledged by the animal kingdom.

If evil is defined as what is destructive to life, then natural evil, such as tornados and hurricanes, seem to be an integral part of the natural order. It is said that we couldn't have the world as it is without them, at least not anything like the structure of physics that we have. But that presumes that God is not almighty, that he was unable to create the world without natural evil in it. What else is he unable to do?

With the exception of some evident chaos and turbulence in nature, the generally consistent order to the universe enables mankind to create and progress technologically. When I left seminary in 1961, I went to Michigan to teach and work off a major in mathematics part time. As I moved through the two year sequence in calculus and analytic geometry, and beyond that into differential equations, I was astounded at the absolute logic and precision of mathematics and the world that it reflected. My subsequent studies in physics left me in further awe of the universe. It is a rational work of art. And when I look at the beauty of nature, and realize the magnificent intricacies of physics and mathematics that lie behind even so simple a thing as a snowflake, it is all the more astonishingly beautiful. God must be a romantic [rather than a square] as well as a logician, to have created the world as it is.

In advanced mathematics we were warned to follow the rules of logic rather than common sense - which could lead us astray, because many of the problems dealt with figures or situations which were uncommon. After all common sense is just the acquired learning about common experiences, and when you go beyond the range of common experiences, such as in the macroscopic or microscopic, or deal with speeds significantly above common speeds, then common sense does not apply. In those ranges of learning you run into uncommon-sensical truths such as that space is curved. However, it is just as non-sensical to think of it as straight. Or take the principle that "time" for an object slows down increasingly proportional to the increase in speed. That is to say, time decreases in an accelerated inverse proportion to the increase in speed. On the other hand, mass increases increasingly proportional to the increase in speed. It's all absurd. And as Joao Magueijo notes in regard to the Big Bang Theory of the universe, "After all, what happened before the Big Bang? In effect, What banged?" [p. 230 of, Faster Than the Speed of Light].

In graduate level mathematics the nth dimensional systems were like a fantasy land, true, but so far beyond the range of everyday experience that it was like another world. Yet it is an integral part of our world of science as it is, and part of the explanation of the world as we know it. In light of the sheer complexity of the universe, and the incredible "luck of the draw" combination of critical factors, Stephen Hawking, a world-class cosmologist, wrote, "it would be very difficult to explain why the universe should have begun in this way, except as an act of a God who intended to create beings like us." And so I wonder as I wander, confident, as the saying goes that, "Out of this world I cannot fall."

26

FIVE

For some reason the trail seems to be fanning out now, but it's hard to tell for sure because there is noticeably less light. And the part I simply cannot understand is how I could have totally miscalculated the time factor. The hard reality that I must face is that the sun is down now. "How could I have erred this much?" Perhaps the trail markers were wrong, and it is really a mile up on this trail, and two miles down on the other. Some practical joker could have turned the signs, for there were several trails leading off from where I began. But that still doesn't explain the sun setting so early that the time to sundown was half what I thought it would be. Maybe my wrist watch is a half hour slow. That would explain it.

I still remember the time when I was in the aviation cadet corps of the U.S. Air Force. One time when I climbed into the pilot's seat, with the instructor behind me, for some reason I didn't want to go up that day, and I was hoping that it would be a short flight. But I didn't have any say in the matter. After the take off, we went through one maneuver after another, as usual. And after a little while the instructor asked over the earphones what time it was. I told him, and we proceeded with the maneuvers. I rarely had the opportunity to fly an airplane in a straight line.

A little later he asked again what time it was, and I told him. This went on another time or two, and all of the time I really preferred to take the plane back and land it.

Then his voice came booming over the earphones in an irritated manner, "Your watch has stopped!" And I immediately checked the fuel gauge.

He wasn't half as irritated as I was about that watch. I have that kind of luck occasionally, and maybe this is one of those times. It could be that the sun sets here earlier than in the lowlands. We crossed a mountain ridge on the drive here, and probably that ridge projecting into the western horizon, combined with the heavy overcast, could slice an hour off of the time when the sun sets. That would explain it, and consequently it is all my fault for not figuring that in. It is the reason I'm in this difficult situation now.

Free will certainly does get us into problem situations where we have to take the consequences of our sins or mistakes, and I guess, after a fashion, a sinful act could be regarded as a mistake with moral overtones. Apparently the consequences are the present time accountability for our actions in a moral universe. After all, people are prone to rationalizing away any guilt, or long term accountability. The very capacity to make mistakes, as well as good achievements, or to have a materially shaping effect on the context in which we exist, is a God-given dual gift of accountability and creativity, or else of destructiveness, depending on the bias of the will. Like a lot of things, free will comes to us as a two-edged sword; it can cut either way.

But in a mystical sense the material world is just the medium in which spirits interact with each other. Materiality gives concreteness to our actions, and time gives a context of continuity, and consequently accountability. It is fitting that relativity physics regards time as interrelated with mass and speed. Consequently time is a very this worldly thing, a factor unique to this space-time framework. It is appropriate that the Bible speaks of the eternity of God as timeless – that "With the Lord a day is like a thousand years, and a thousand years are like a day." (II Peter 3:8) God is without beginning or end, for earth time is unique to this material world. There is a logical sense then in which the present moment of time rests in the eternity of God. Consequently the eternity of God is as close to us as the present moment of time. As St. Paul would say, "In him we live and move and have our being." (Acts 17:28) That's a comforting thought, particularly now for me.

Maybe the desk clerk erred when he told me the time of sunset.

SIX

It's easier going now; the trail is flatter here. Up ahead through the trees the light seems to be just a shade brighter, and a line of red light on the horizon. "The horizon! I must be at the crest of the mountain ridge now."

I have to walk slower now, picking my steps carefully in this very dim light; I don't want to wander off the other side of the ridge in the dark. I can just barely see it a dozen feet ahead now. As I move closer, I'm even with the line of trees at the edge of the ridge; the land before me slopes steeply down out of sight in the darkness. I seem to be on a cliff, or something mighty close to it. Not exactly the safest place in the world to be, with snow on the ground as night falls.

Standing here I feel very sad as the darkness falls gently about me – odd that it seems gentle. The words of St. Paul echo in the back of my mind, "In him we live and move and have our being." (Acts 17:28) There's a comfort in that. The slim dull red line of light on the western horizon before me barely silhouettes the mountain ridges in the distance, then slowly fades out, and vanishes.

Looking up in the night sky there is not a star to be seen, nor the moon to be found; there must be a heavy overcast. Yet, some starlight must be filtering through the clouds for I can just barely see the trees beside me; I seem to be able to dimly make out objects to a distance of a dozen feet;

beyond that it fades into blackness modified by a haze of white lying below it.

"Thank God for the snow." If it were not for the snow reflecting what little light comes through, I would be lost in impenetrable darkness.

"I wish that I were back at the lodge now, lounging before that huge fireplace. I would give several hundred dollars to be able to trade this place for that one. Then, as I wished to, I could occasionally venture out on the balcony for a few minutes to look at the winter night and the frozen river way below at the foot of the ridge."

The soft creak of a tree brings me back to the harsh reality of the here and now, and reminds me that magical wishes are not granted in this world that is sometimes burdened with sin and grief, and besides, there is no star to wish upon.

It is time to face the grim reality that confronts me. Foolishness got me into this situation, but unless I act with great care there can be grim consequences for me. I am alone, without human companionship, and it is a dark winter night as I stand at the very top of a snow-covered mountain ridge. "How could I have been so stupid?" The trip down is going to be difficult and extremely treacherous.

I need to take account of what assets I have against the journey that lies before me. At least I am warmly dressed: combat boots and wool stockings, long winter underwear, blue jeans, ski sweater, wool skull cap, nylon parka, and lined leather gloves. There is no problem there. At least I had the good sense to dress for the climb.

In the zippered pocket of my parka I feel the three books of paper matches and the compass that I had placed there in case of emergency, but the compass is useless to me now that night has fallen. It's a comfort to feel the hunting knife in its sheath at my side. All in all, I'm well equipped for the descent. That's a consolation. Also, I'm in good physical shape because of being a physical fitness nut.

With care I can make the descent without stopping to build a fire and waiting for a search party. That would be a humiliating thing to do – to be defeated by the situation. Actually, there is nobody at the lodge who can come, except the desk clerk, cook, and a few waitresses. I have nobody but myself to blame for the predicament that I am in. It would be nice if I could blame somebody else; a fatalistic philosophy would certainly be convenient now. But individual human responsibility is central to Judaism and Christianity, and despite the favorite theological sport of trying to hang the responsibility on God for all human mistakes and evil, nevertheless, in the end, and even now, every person is responsible for his own actions. Even though there are heavily influencing factors on the human will, such as genetic inheritance, childhood upbringing, life experiences, the external situation, the emotion of the moment, and the culture. Nevertheless the will is a free agent — free to oppose those influences by the time of adulthood.

Ethically, the bias of the will – and most essentially to love or hate – must initially begin by the person's own choice, by a conscious or unconscious act of the will. The judgment, or reward, in the situation depends on how much of that initial bias of the will is inclined toward the self. A reinforcing, a sort of feedback influence, or conditioning seems to occur as time goes by.

A person could even think of the bias of the will as essentially toward good or evil, and perhaps even as a momentum that continually increases as each act of the will adds to it. Consequently, the farther along in life a person goes, the more difficult it is to change that direction. Sometimes a crisis in life will give a reflection of what that person has allowed himself to become, and make clear the dire need to change.

It's harder to change the farther one has gone in life; the hardness is sort of a partial judgment for accumulated sins, after all there is no such thing as cheap grace. And the hardness of change is a protection when the fundamental bias is good. And even if a person could trace the initial bias to a subconscious choice, nevertheless it is the person's own subconscious that made the decision. It is a part of him, and he must take responsibility if it progresses into action. All acts (acts of the will) must pass the approval of the conscious mind, the ego, the arbiter between the self and the external real world. It is in that monitoring phase that final responsibility lies.

Of course a case could be made that the unconscious is only repressed and suppressed consciousness. And that what we conceive of as the conscious mind is only a mental construct of learned natural and social consistencies that the mind erects in order to deal with the real world beyond the self. What is remembered then in times of waking consciousness is just what is able to pass through a pattern or grid of consistencies that are essential in interaction with the world outside the self.

The conscious mind then would be regarded as a subset of the total set of remembrances, the unconscious being the remainder of them, with the capacity to reason and to will included. That mental construct subsides during sleep because it is no longer needed, and then the free flow of mental activity during sleep is not remembered upon awakening, except as a dream if for some reason it is directed to the consciousness as a message.

Such a construct or grid, that defines the self in relation to the world, evidently is related to heart rate, and in turn to muscular tension. For the mind continually monitors what goes on around the person, for example thunder will not wake me up at night (unless it is in my block, near at hand), but a mosquito buzzing near the bed will wake me up.

The waking is a call to action, and the reality construct goes into place. Both the conscious and unconscious mind normally co-operate, for example everybody probably has had the experience, while driving a car, that their center, or focus, of consciousness wandered off in thought on some concern, and miles later their attention returns to the driving. Who "minded the store" while they were "out to lunch?" Their unconscious did; and it performed the very sophisticated feat of driving the car – which is not a trained reflex. Let some unusual thing occur on the road or in the traffic, and full attention immediately returns to the driving.

SEVEN

Turning to the right now, and staying back a half a dozen feet from the edge of the ridge, I follow the trail that leads down to the lodge. In a manner of speaking, it is time now to go down into the valley of the shadow of death. And it irks me that I have to go it alone. But, I can get myself off the mountain safely, even in this kind of weather. I grew up in it, and winter in Indiana was always fascinating to me. But I probably will never live this venture down.

The trail is rather level here! But it is twice as long as the trail up, therefore it must meander a lot. "Wait! There is no squeak to the snow when I step on it. And the trees are not dripping. That indicates the temperature is probably in the upper twenties, or lower." That adds another element of danger to the situation; however, so far the journey has been rather pleasant.

Life isn't always pleasant. It is a cost of living that we sometimes take the brunt of other peoples' sins and mistakes, as well as our own. Human evil is a fact of life. But America has not had a concept of evil for a long time – not in the sense of willful and deliberate evil. It always seems to be regarded either as something that can be voted out come next election time, or else as something so unreal that it can be regarded as a sickness and included under the heading of neurosis or psychosis.

I believe that a person can consciously and deliberately make a morally wrong decision for the sake of personal gain of wealth or power. As individuals, people vary all over the scale as self-seeking and even combative. History certainly suggests that. I would estimate that 95% of recorded history has been spent with a war going on some place.

George Bernard Shaw was correct in stating that war is what mankind does best of all. And only by the conviction of an idea can a person transcend it. People haven't changed much since his time, despite public education; the literacy level in the twentieth century may have been higher than in any previous century, yet it was the bloodiest century of them all.

Adolf Hitler was an extremely well-read and cultured man; and it is strange how people prefer to regard him as sick, rather than evil. Maybe it is because to admit that he was evil gets far too close to home, for the seeds of evil – pride in all of its various forms, is present in all of us to one degree or another.

There apparently is a dualism of good and evil in this world, and the disconcerting thing is that it exists in all of us. There is a natural inclination to sin for two reasons. First, because we were born into a context of sin we are influenced by it. Second, the temptations make their entry through the vulnerability of the senses (natural concupiscence); that is the basic avenue of appeal. But all sin is based on pride – the inordinate love of self more than God, and more than others.

Explaining it or naming it really doesn't help much, if at all. It seems that religion has been the only means by which people have been able to transcend that inclination to sinning, and even with that, the result varies considerably.

But this is hardly the time to muse about that. I need to pay more attention to the trail; it's sloping down more now and requires a little more attention. There is a drop-off to my left, and I can see nothing but blackness below the edge – which I need to avoid at all costs. So to speak, this literally is "living on the edge."

EIGHT

"It just can't be!" The trail slopes down into a crevice, and the rock walls rise abruptly from the trail. It looks horribly dark in there, and I kneel down to examine the snow to make sure that is where the trail leads. Unfortunately the trail does lead into it, so there's no place to go but straight ahead.

As I enter the crevice it is so totally dark that I keep the palms of my hands against the rock walls, which are not even a yard apart, and sometimes only two feet apart. Each step now is made gingerly for fear of a drop-off. In this darkness even a one foot drop-off could cause injury if I were unaware of it before I stepped.

There doesn't seem to be any end to the crevice. In some ways the touch of the cold walls is comforting – I certainly can't slip and fall sideways, but on the other hand they seem threatening and seem to loom over me. Looking up, for all the world it seems like a cave because I can't really distinguish a lighter slot of sky above.

The crevice seems to narrow here, and I turn slightly sideways in order to move ahead. "Of all the screwball situations to get myself into, I can really pick them! Surely the thing doesn't dead end here?" After a few yards of very cautious movement I come to where the fissure widens out again to almost a yard wide. I can dimly see ahead a slot of dark gray in relief against the blackness that surrounds me.

Encouraged by the hope that the end of this narrow passage way is in sight, I walk just a little faster. Now the end of the crevice becomes more distinct, and appears to be only twenty or thirty feet ahead.

There's a slight sense of relief that grows as I traverse the last distance of the passageway. Coming out now into the night, the snow almost seems bright by comparison. Apparently my eyes had become a lot more dark-adapted in the crevice. Ahead, the snow covered ground rises just thirty or forty feet away, far too steep to climb in this snow. I know better than to turn left; about a dozen feet or less, the land slopes so steeply down out of sight that the only thing that can be seen is a velvet blackness. To the right, on the same level as I am, there are some trees just forty or fifty feet away, and it is evident from the tracks in the snow that the trail goes that way. It is easy going also since the trail is pretty much level. It is a relief to be going in that direction, away from the cliff.

It seems like a surrealistic situation. Behind me, for all practical purposes, is nothingness, and on each side, about fifteen feet away, are snow covered rock walls. Ahead are some trees. After about ten or fifteen feet I stop. "Something has changed! I can sense it, but not name it." Looking up on an impulse, I can see fifteen to twenty feet above and in front of me the narrow natural rock bridge that this area of the mountain ridge is famous for. Apparently there was a subtle change in what little light there is just as I was about to pass under the bridge. I can barely make out the outline of it in this darkness. It would have been much nicer to have seen it in the sunlight, especially with this snow on it.

But, I need to hurry on, and as I enter the woods the trail begins to slope downwards slightly. Turning around briefly I try to distinguish the natural bridge silhouetted against the night sky. But at this distance of thirty or more feet, it is almost impossible to make it out, and I resume my journey.

Either the overcast has lightened or else my eyes have become more dark-adapted for I can distinguish trees at a distance of fifty feet or more, and I can see where the trail turns slightly to the left about thirty feet ahead. According to my sense of direction, and every turn that I have kept track of, the trail is headed in generally the right direction, within ten degrees. Of course I can expect meanders and switch-backs that will alternately take me off course, but at least I seem to be on the right trail.

There is a strange sense of unity with nature now, I am alert to every change in the firmness of the snow beneath me, and to every occasional creak of a tree. It doesn't feel cold at all, even though the trees don't drip anymore and I know that the temperature is below freezing. It really is rather relaxing walking along here in the snow. I only wish that I didn't need to hurry back to the lodge. It would be fascinating to take it slow and easy and absorb all of the majestic quiet beauty of this snowy landscape.

There's an unusual feeling of belongingness here. It's me up against nature here in order to survive, and yet I don't feel any againstness now. I would have thought that nature, in a situation such as this, would appear to be harsh and cruel. But there is none of that. There is a sense of gentleness to it, a sense of almost being "at home" in the woods, and a profound sense of the presence and care of God. The words come to mind,

> In him [God] we live and move and have our being.

And I wonder if perhaps St. Paul, in all of his various journeys and hardships, had experienced the same feelings I do. Perhaps his frequent trips and consequent nearness to nature - and through it to God - was one source of his sense of the ubiquity of God [the every-whereness of God], and consequently of St. Paul's frequently expressed confidence that "God is faithful" – that you can depend on him; he will live up to his promises.

That is still important. In the world as St. Paul knew it there were only two dimensions of materiality that he usually encountered — first, the world of nature, which he perceived as created by God, and second, the world of people, - whom he believed are created in the image of God. [According to Piere Teilhard deChardin, that famous, yet undefined "image of God," is the capacity to turn the mind back upon itself in moral self-reflection]. True the image of God in fallen mankind is blurred and warped as a consequence of being born into a context of sin; I think that is where the bias of the will came from that puts mankind in a state of rebellion against God. Nevertheless, both of those factors are related to the act of creation.

We tend to live in our synthetic world of things as a defense against the unpredictable events of nature, such as the weather. And the very order of the universe is used to create our own environment, and so in one more sense Jesus' words are true,

Jesus answered them, "Is it not written in your Law, 'I have said you are gods?' If he called them 'gods' to whom the word of God came – and the Scripture cannot be broken – what about the one whom the Father set apart as his very own and sent into the world?"

(John 10:34-36a)

The efforts of mankind that have increased our isolation from nature and its vicissitudes, seems to bring with it an increasing sense of independence and distance from God. And people tend to go their own way and do their own thing. Order in the universe is used through technology as a way of increasing our independence from God by creating our own manner of life. But I think situation ethics, where every person is a law unto himself, has resulted in a moral decay and even criminality in most nations, including this one. The result reminds me of the reported occasion when Napoleon was accused of stealing the crown of France. His answer was, "I didn't steal it! I found it lying in the gutter!" That has ominous possibilities here.

With the world problems we have – and some of them are life threatening on a massive and even cataclysmic scale – the future is tenuous. Europe is in the throes of the effects of mass migrations that have occurred over several decades, and that are disruptive socially, culturally, economically, politically, and militarily.

Today with TV bringing the image of the face, as well as the voice, into the home, it has vastly changed politics. Since the impact of TV advertisements has had much success in generating sales for businesses, then by the same principle of influence, it has a subtle and critical impact on the manner of government, or at least the success or failure of a candidate for office. Of course there are variations of effect of the media, that vary from individual to individual, and that sometimes springs from the generally sinful character of the "City of Men," as St. Augustine termed secular human society. People, by our fallen nature, cannot always be good, even if the situation is good. History teaches us that, and so does Scripture. Even redeemed mankind – those of the true Church Militant — do not reach perfection in this earthly phase of existence. Because of free will, we too are susceptible to influence from the world of people who live and love in opposition to the will of God – and today, flaunt it in the face of God.

But there is in this present time the beauty of God's creation, and as the theology of the High Middle Ages affirmed, there is some vestige of God in every aspect of creation. Here now I walk among the gentle beauty of God's creation, and sense a one-ness with all that God created. Even the snow does not feel like a threat, but is soft and seems to have a gentleness to it.

But all of that is a heavy mind trip, and I need to focus on surviving this trip down the mountain, and coming through it all unharmed. That will be challenge enough for this day. At least it feels like an easy and pleasant challenge – like having the wind at my back.

NINE

The trail is becoming steeper now in its downward slope, and seems to turn slightly more to the left – the ridge rises to my left. I can see dimly ahead that a spur of the ridge seems to block the way in the distance, and to my right the ground rises. Somewhere ahead and below, the trail must turn right, but where? I simply can't see now where it turns, for at much over a few hundred feet it all fades into blackness over white. It gives a strange sense of descent into the unknown, yet at the same time a real curiosity to see what's ahead, at the bend of the trail – a reality that must eventually be confronted.

With the trail steeper now I have to walk slower; besides, this is no time for surprises, what with the territory totally unknown to me. And yet, there really is no fear. It would be pretentious to chalk it up as "the courage to be," and yet there must be some of that to it. No thanks to me though; it comes from a basic trust in the goodness and presence of God. As far back as I can remember, there has been a sense of that, but in many ways now it is less than when I was a child.

Perhaps that was what Jesus was referring to when he said,

> I tell you, whoever does not accept the kingdom of God like a child will never enter it.
>
> (Mark 10:15)

Apparently it takes the humility of unquestioning trust. I still remember how that as a kid in the early years of grade school I always wanted to go with my two older brothers on their paper route when it was storming. In the spring and summer in Indiana there would be violent electrical storms, and to me that was the thrill par excellence — to be right out in it, and to watch the magnificent displays of lightning, and to hear the thunder roll. As the saying goes, "It is the sound of God moving furniture in heaven." It never occurred to me that I could get hurt, after all it was God's world, and I was one of his children. And the church had told me of his care for me. It must have been right for I was never hurt, and my faith was vindicated — but to say that cynically now would avoid the pragmatic fact that indeed my faith was vindicated by my own personal history.

It was always worth it then to get soaking wet — I even enjoyed that part — the cool driving rain — and to see the lightning flash, and nature go wild. I never doubted the goodness of God. The violence of the storms was just his way of reminding us that he is still here and in charge, by providing a little beauty in extravagant display. The years haven't changed me all that much. I still get a thrill out of watching a storm. I even got a kick out of a hurricane in Florida when the eye of the storm passed over the house where I lived; it was a fascinating experience.

But there have been times when I have questioned the goodness of God. History in school made me do that. But it was a bum rap. The sins of mankind are just that — the sins of mankind, not God's. The answer to the whole puzzle came to me in seminary. Ever since the first fall of mankind when people went their own way and did their own thing, there has been evil in this world, but it was evil that came by their choice. What essentially distinguishes people from the animal kingdom is that ability to turn the mind back upon itself in moral self reflection, and therefore have the capacity for deliberate, willful choice of good or evil. The capacity to know both good and evil apparently is a god -like characteristic; as the Genesis account records:

> And the Lord God said, "The man has now become like one of us, knowing good and evil."
> (Genesis 3:22a)

God knew evil intellectually, as that which was destructive of life, and therefore against his will. Although mankind learned of evil experientially in the fall, in the process he acquired more of the perspective of God. Some theologians speak of it as "a fall upwards." However, I think the cost is too high in consequences, for example 40 million casualties in World War II alone.

There seems to be a moral decay that sets in, which a person cannot correct on his own. The person bears the memory and consequences of sin, which together can have a deteriorating effect which seems to be inevitable. There seems to be a moral grain to the universe which we go against at our own peril. It is the natural law that St. Paul wrote of which the Gentiles knew by nature, and the Jews knew by revelation. In regard to the moral law of God, as the old saying goes,

> You don't break the Ten Commandments;
> You only break yourself upon them.

When we transgress the moral Law of God, and take the consequences, there is an alienation that tends to develop of man from God, not God from man. The attitude of God towards mankind has always been that of love ("agape," an unwillingness to do without). As it is said, "God is faithful." We can count on him.

The word "love" in English has come to have so many meanings that it is almost meaningless, except to denote "attraction," as opposed to repulsion. However, in the Greek language of New Testament times, "agape" had the meaning of "an unwillingness to do without." That puts it in straight English, without using sentimental words that vary in meaning from person to person, depending on their personal history. It is a comforting thing to know that the attitude of God towards mankind is based on a more stable, enduring thing than emotion or feelings. Feelings are a composite response made up of genetically inherited temperament, the fleeting emotion of the moment, the influence of the external situation, and previous experiences. But, "God is faithful." You can trust him; he lives up to his word. On the other hand, to let your feelings be your guide can sometimes result in your being in prison. After all, murder is sometimes a crime of passion.

Of course, the attitude of God towards mankind is a problem to some people today. After all, in the case of the prophets telling us of God's love for people – words that came by revelation are still only words. And everybody knows that "talk is cheap." Therefore, unless a person accepts the validity and integrity of Scripture, then such words are just that, words.

Once it is accepted that the nature of Jesus is deity, then there is no question about God's love for people. We can trust that the attitude of God towards mankind is one of love. We can trust that he believes in us, more than we believe in him, and so much so that he is "unwilling to do without" us, even though a lot of people are willing to do without him.

But enough of the mind trip. I need to focus on the task at hand – the task, the challenge of getting off of this mountain alive.

TEN

The ridge on my left seems to tower over me, and it rises steeply from the left side of the path. To the right, the ground rises sharply and curves convexly so that I can't see the top of it. Ahead, but nearer now, the spur of the ridge looms in front of me. It all concurs to give a curious sense of engulfment by the situation, not in a threatening sense, but in an awe-inspiring sense, like being held "in the hollow of God's hand" – reminiscent of the line, "For in him we live and move and have our being."

There is a profound significance to that statement of St. Paul's, for according to it, God is the context in which each of us live; he is a presence as close as the air we breathe.

The ubiquity and immediacy of God – the every-whereness and right-nowness of God, is an astonishing concept. When a person confronts the reality of it; it means that we can relax in life without fear of falling out of this world, for underneath are the everlasting arms. And that when the tour of duty that constitutes life on this earth is over, then there is a going home, for here, in this material dimension of life, as spirits we are but

> strangers or passing travelers on earth,
> looking for a country of their own,
> longing for a better country, I mean, the heavenly
>   one.

(Hebrews 11:13b, 14b, 16b)

After a fashion then, life on this earth is a way of being born for eternity. The physical aspect of life is like a limitation on life until it comes of age, and the material world is the medium for the interaction of spirits, a training ground for character, an opportunity for a new born spirit to choose God, or go his own way before he progresses to the strictly spiritual level of existence.

According to the Genesis account mankind was created for fellowship with God. The time of the choice is this earthly phase of existence. Anything as transcendent in being and power as God himself can only be comprehended by us now in our finiteness by the concreteness of the earthly life of the Son of God, deity incarnate, who is the exact image of God the Father. (Hebrews 1:1-4) We too, with Philip the Apostle, must accept that because of our own limitations, and because there is a justice in God requiring the consistency of faith and commitment, there must be a proof of our integrity of commitment shown by life lived in the faith before there can be a confirming religious experience. Besides, I think most people would treat with disregard any unexpected spiritual experience by rushing to a psychiatrist to rationalize it away.

For those who go their own way and do their own thing, God simply ratifies their free choice, and grants life outside of his presence. But in that state there is unrestrained evil, all of the Adolf Hitlers of this world, with no restraints except themselves. That will be hell, worse than any that could be conceived or administered by God.

But enough of that flight of thought. The uniqueness and grandeur of my present environment should not be wasted by lack of attention, for it isn't often that I find a quiet place with the solitude necessary to ponder such topics. But I need to hustle now. If I don't speed up, and the time gets much later than this, there is bound to be a search party, and that would be an extreme embarrassment to me.

The quiet beauty of this place, and the uniqueness of it is awesome. It reminds me of the statement by Ernest Hemmingway,

"This world is a fine place, and worth fighting for."

ELEVEN

Ever since several early failures in life, I have tried to train courage into myself. After all, it has been said that, "Life isn't anything except opportunity – opportunity to be something, or do something." Maybe that is one of the underlying reasons why I am on this mountain – in the dark, in the snow, the cold, and alone. And the memories flood my mind, "Precious memories, how they linger, how they fill my soul with joy."

I remember back in 1954 sitting in the rear of a C-119 Troop Carrier airplane on a trip to an army base in Georgia. The loud drone and vibration of the engines was monotonous. The seat isn't very comfortable either, just an aluminum tubular frame covered with a webbing and hinged to the side of the plane – not exactly first class passage, but then it wasn't designed to be; it was built for paratroopers. I was told that these C-119s were loud, and they were right; but I wasn't told how uncomfortable the seats were. Of course, with the back-pack parachute on, it makes it difficult to sit down, and I can't lean my head against the fuselage of the airplane. It's the first time I have had this type of parachute on. I'm accustomed to the seat-pack type, which I used when piloting an airplane. They were more comfortable than these because a person sat on the parachute, and could lean against the seat-back.

Here in the cargo pod the accommodations may not be great, but there is one consolation, in the terrible event of a crash, the front end of the airplane hits first, and presumably takes the worst of the crash. "This thing looks huge. I wonder what its capacity is?" Looking it over is kind of interesting. I've never been in this type of plane before. On each side of the central fuselage, there is a separate fuselage that is just large enough to house one large radial, reciprocating engine. Those two fuselages rest on the wings, and are connected at, and jointly form, the tail of the plane. There is a wide door on each side of the cargo area, where the paratroopers jump out. About seven feet up on each side of the plane there is a cable that runs along the inside of the plane; it is the cable which the static lines on the parachutes hook onto. Paratroopers don't have to be concerned with when to pull the rip cord. The static line does it for them.

The chute I have on doesn't have a static line. Instead there is a D ring on the end of the ripcord at the left side of my chest. It is comforting in light of the sheer dangerousness of life, or at least life as it has been for almost a year now. To make matters worse, in this year of 1954 we seem to be right at the brink of war every now and then, with frequent trouble in Berlin, and shooting across the 38th Parallel nearly every day in Korea.

Dan looks pretty bored over on the other side of the plane. We left Oklahoma in too much of a hurry to think to bring along a deck of cards to pass the time with. I should have bought a pack in Charleston last night when we stopped over night at the air base there. But we should be coming to Georgia pretty soon. We probably are about over the mountains now. Standing up it feels good to stretch, even though the parachute harness is constricting. When it is used it has to be on so tight you can hardly stand erect, otherwise it will shuck you out when the parachute opens.

The window isn't very big, and the plexiglas is heavily scored by sand on the outside, and smeared, probably by engine oil. It is difficult to see through it. Below, the terrain looks like mountains totally covered by forests. But it is difficult trying to see out of these windows.

Maybe if I lay down on the long rack seat, with my parachute under my back, and another one used as a pillow for my head and shoulders, plus one to hold my legs and feet even with my body, I might be able to get some sleep. The three parachutes in a row level out the sag of the webbing of the rack seat. I just hope that lying on my parachute doesn't affect the ability of it to open. However, as I remember the way they are packed, and the way they open, it shouldn't impair it. Besides, the adjustment in the accommodations is a lot more comfortable than it was. Even the loud drone of the engines is a reassuring sound; it is a lot more restful than it would be if I didn't hear them.

I have often wished that I could see what lay ahead in the future, but as fast paced as things often have been in this last year, I guess it's a blessing not to be able to see ahead. It's often a full time job just taking it one day at a time. In fact, the very uncertainty of life makes it exciting. It puts a once-for-allness stake on some events of each day. It makes it a challenge, not a problem. Just like in snow skiing, you have to lean into life, and not shrink from it. A year ago I would never have guessed that today I would be over the Appalachians in a troop carrier airplane.

I have had some exciting surprises, and this is one of them. But on the other hand, there have been some great disappointments, and it is just as well that I didn't know about them ahead of time; the memory of them is bad enough as it is. As one gospel song goes,

I don't know what the future holds,
but I know who holds the future.

There seems to be a basic trust in life that comes with the Christian faith. That can be a critical factor that enables a person to do many things, and face the basic anxieties of life that otherwise can be both time and soul consuming.

I notice that the relentless drone of the engines is relaxing in a way; it sort of envelopes a person in a low strong monotone and vibration. It really is kind of restful, and the airplane is so big that I don't feel cramped for space.

Hearing the forward hatch to the cockpit open, I turn to see who's coming. The flight engineer appears through the doorway and descends the short ladder to the deck. He doesn't seem to notice my non-regulation use of two parachutes. He walks awkwardly – because of his parachute harness – to the door on my side of the plane. He braces himself, hanging onto the frame of the plane with one hand while he opens the door with the other, and pulls it to him and fastens it to the inside of the plane. Evidently we must be approaching the army base in Georgia, our destination. The side doors are opened at about one or two thousand feet up prior to landing, so that if anything goes wrong you merely have to run out the door without having to pause to open it, presuming of course that you already have your parachute on. That way there is no time wasted in putting it on. If the emergency occurs on landing you can get out quickly too. Likewise, on take-off the doors are left open until the plane is up a few thousand feet.

The flight engineer moves cautiously to the opposite side of the plane, and with even more care opens that door. I guess in the back of his mind he must feel the double jeopardy of his position, what with two open doors. But the open doors don't appear to cause any noticeable suction on him. The plane must be down to 150 mph or less; nevertheless, with good reason he exercises a great deal of caution as he moves toward the center of the plane, and then forward to the hatch to the cockpit area.

"How about that!" There wasn't any noticeable suction from the open doorway. It's worth a quick look outside. I could sure see better out of one of those wide doorways than through one of these small scratched windows.

Getting up from this position with a parachute on turns out to be something of a problem; I nearly have to roll out of the rack. As I stand up I tighten up my parachute harness so that I can barely stand erect. If I wind up going out the door I don't want to be shucked out of this thing when the chute opens.

Dan, my friend on the other side of the plane, looks at me a little puzzled, apparently wondering what I'm up to. I yell over to him, "I'm going to take a look outside." Then I turn, and start toward the open door on my side of the plane. About six feet this side of it I grab a frame member on the side of the plane, and hold onto it as I move slowly toward the doorway. At the side of the doorway I move a step toward the center of the plane, still holding on to the frame member with my left hand, and then turn facing the doorway with my feet over two feet apart and grab the other side of the doorway with my right hand. Spread-eagled like this in front of the opening I really don't feel any suction, and the view is absolutely fantastic. Below me is nothing but a deep carpet of green trees that rolls over the hills as far as I can see. It must be Georgia. So that's what it's like. There's an awful lot of forest land down there. Looking up I see the right fuselage, and above it is nothing but blue sky; it's a beautiful day outside, and this is the best vantage point in the whole airplane. Watching the hills and trees move slowly by with nothing but sky between us is an exhilarating experience.

"Oh, no! It's too early and too high up for him to be making a turn into the landing pattern." Nevertheless, the carpet of green trees below me is slowly shifting to directly in front of me as the C-119 rolls lazily over on its right side in preparation for entry into the pattern. And the forest scene in front of me starts to rotate as the turn begins.

It strikes me that I'm in a mighty peculiar position, spread-eagled face down over a large opening several thousand feet up. One slip, and I'll be walking back to the base, dragging the parachute — if it opens, that is. I hope laying on it didn't impair it any. Chances are they'd court-martial me for putting myself in a position where I wind up going out the door without authorization.

It's kind of fascinating though, watching the forest in front of me rotating as the plane rounds the turn. It was sort of worth the risk, even though I had no intention of still being here when the pilot turned the plane.

The rotation gradually stops, and the forest begins to sink slowly from in front of me to below me as the plane comes out of its bank. The plane settles down to level flight. Figuring that the first turn in the pattern may not be very many minutes away, I move away from the door by reverse process, and return to my seat.

The very technology of mankind — the capacity for which is a gift from God — enables us to experience life more widely and intensely than we could without it. Without it, it would not be possible to get a bird's eye view of a Georgia forest. Such possibilities of experience are just another manifestation of the "grace" of God, in other words, the unmerited favor of God. [In straight English, grace is defined as "the unmerited favor of God."]

Here on the mountain, I could use some more of that grace along about now – in deliverance, for I am now very conscious of the passing of time, and the risk that Maria would recruit a search party. And the lodge is nowhere in sight. Around me now there is just the darkness, and the beautiful, relentless whiteness of the snow.

But I have promises to keep,
And miles to go before I sleep,
And miles to go before I sleep.

. . . . .

Robert Frost, "Stopping by Woods on a Snowy Evening"

TWELVE

Turning my thoughts to the present physical situation, I notice that the spur of the ridge that extends across in front of me looms closer now, and I can see that I'm coming to a turn in the trail. Just thirty feet ahead the trail turns to the right. That should put me more in line with the lodge. At this juncture of the spur with the ridge, it is like being in the furrow of a mountain, enfolded by the forest, and yet at the same time being a free agent, for I'm the only mobile living thing that I have seen in the forest this evening. Yet the forest seems to have a quiet aliveness to it; and there is a sense of comradery-ness to it, as if we're in this together, or rather as if I'm a welcome guest passing through its domain. There is a curious sense of parity with it; as if it is no threat to me.

There is a striking polarity to the natural world; it has a dualism to it – light and darkness, north and south magnetic poles, positive and negative charges on particles. It is strange to me how people in modern day rationalism react so violently at the thought of such dualism extending over into the spiritual dimension of reality in the dichotomy of good and evil.

I don't think that evil can be rationalized away as just a lack of goodness. Human history has always had a more aggressive characteristic to it than merely the passive absence of good. In the lives of ones like Rasputin and Adolf Hitler, they seem to have been too evil to have become that way just by the absence of good. It took some diligence and plenty of outside help from an active, personal force of evil at loose in history.

Of course, rationalism arbitrarily and presumptuously, by faith, denies the existence of the spiritual dimension of reality, an assertion that cannot be proven. Angels are dismissed as imaginary, and while virtually denying that there is the dimension of spiritual reality, still there usually is the token admission that God exists. Yet, if that is admitted then it opens the door to the conclusion of the existence of the spiritual dimension of reality. Besides, if there is natural law, who passed the law? That's why modern scientists speak of "natural consistencies." Added to that, they now have to take into consideration, randomness, turbulence, and chaos in the universe. And as Hawking, a world famous cosmologist put it, In the Big Bang Theory of Evolution, "What banged?"

Once God's existence is admitted, then it is no further stretch of the imagination, and no new principle need be admitted, to accept the plausibility of the existence of angels. Once that is conceded, then the fall of an angel, just as mankind fell, is feasible. And Jesus' reference to Satan as the Prince of this world becomes a sobering concept. Contrary to the insurance companies, in the first two chapters of the book of Job it attributes natural evil – disasters (such as tornados) and disease – to the intrusion of the action of Satan into the operation of nature. I don't notice that anybody else has come up with a better idea.

But if the concept of Satan is dismissed as fictional, then the blame for such arbitrary "natural evils" tends to fall on God, and it throws a very large and heavy question mark over the concept of God's love, and from that a question mark over the validity of the teachings of Jesus, for the one principle of God's love for mankind is central to it. And, of course, the denial of the dimension of spiritual reality under-cuts the reality that Jesus was in any way uniquely the Son of God, or resurrected. It is little wonder then that one Pope stated that the concept of the existence of Satan is basic to Christianity.

One only needs to look at human history for further reason to ponder the concept of a personal force of evil at loose in this world. And wasn't it the world famous psycho-analyst Carl Gustav Jung who said that we have not dealt the devil a mortal blow by calling him neurosis? No! We haven't! There are several serious reasons to consider the words attributed to Jesus about the Prince of this world, because some would call into question the justice of God in creating people, when they look at the evil perpetrated by people on others. The popular means is to make the charge against God specific by pointing to one case of devastating cruelty to a child, such as in a war situation, and then claim that because of that one event, it would have been more just if God had not created people at all, rather than to have let such unhappiness and suffering come upon even just that one child, and there are many more. Regardless of God's reasons for creation, they cannot be vindicated because of that one event. However, because of the next phase of life, which will be eternally in heaven for those who live in faith-ful obedience, "It will be worth it all." And here on the mountain, in "the peace-able kingdom of God", a foretaste of heaven, it will be worth it all.

THIRTEEN

Turning my thoughts back to the present situation, I notice that a turn in the trail lies just ahead, and since this is unknown territory, I am anxious to see what lies ahead. As I round the turn I can see that the trail is straight for about several hundred feet. Apparently the overcast has lightened, or else my eyes have become even more dark adapted than previously, for I can distinctly see the trees at the top of the spur of the ridge on my left, and at the top of the hill on my right. They appear as black against white.

It worries me that Maria may have a search party sent out to help me, for it seems like I have been on the trail a long time. Maybe it wouldn't hurt if I tried jogging for awhile, after all, the trail is only mildly sloped here, and only a little slick, even though the snow is packed on it. My boots have good traction.

After jogging for about forty feet, it occurs to me that what little time I save by jogging isn't worth the added risk of breaking an arm or leg. I slow down to a walk again. Besides, it is too beautiful a place to hurry through it. What a pity I don't have the time to stop occasionally to enjoy the scenery.

It is interesting that the Gospel accounts several times speak of Jesus going off by himself into the hills, apparently to meditate. Being here now, I can understand that. It is curious that he whom we regard as the Son of God would have known what it is like to be hot or cold, hungry or tired. It is notable that the humanity of Jesus is a critical doctrine, for on it rests the atonement – in that he really did die on the cross. Of course, only by going through the experience of physical death could he have been like us in every aspect, and consequently be our sympathetic advocate before God the Father Almighty.

However, in our day the humanity of Christ is not a problem. Most people seem to accept it, but for many the problem arises in accepting the deity of Jesus. They regard him only as a man, a great prophet and teacher, but only a man. Some consider him to be the greatest shaman that ever lived, but stop short of ascribing to him the nature of deity.

Yet the most elemental creed in the New Testament, the critical and most basic statement that distinguishes a true Christian from all other religious persuasions is the simple confession of faith, "Jesus is Lord." That is to say, Deity, sharing the nature of God. Without that nature of deity it would nullify atonement, undercut the authority of his teachings, and make questionable the validity of his promise of eternal life for his disciples. The deity of Jesus is the basic doctrine of the church.

The New Testament is plain in its claims of his deity. In it there is the consistent theme that Jesus is uniquely God's Son. And it usually speaks of him as pre-existent and the incarnate Son of God. From a strictly Biblical point of view – from the ones who walked and talked with Jesus, and saw his miracles and his resurrection, and consequently by the judgment of the early church – his deity is confessed in the primary creed of the church, the Apostles' Creed. He was deity incarnate. Probably one judgment of that truth is that our interpretation of it reflects the very inner core of our being, the inclination of our heart.

Jesus' primary mission when he came into the world – of which he was the instrument of creation – was to reconcile people to God. In one narrative of an incident in a boat on the Sea of Galilee, the winds and the waves [the natural world] recognized him as Lord, even though the people didn't. In telling that story John followed up on a remark he made at the beginning of his account of the gospel, when he stated that Jesus "came unto his own things, and his own people did not receive him." (John 1:11) Just as the Roman Emperor occasionally went on an "adventus," [Latin for "tour of his empire"] so also the Advent of Jesus as Lord and Christ has occurred, and in these in-between times we await his second "appearance" [Greek, "Parousia"] in power and glory for the judgment of all mankind.

To discard the Apostle John's mystical description of the person of Jesus is a presumptuous thing based on a late nineteenth century and early twentieth century rationale that the only reality is material reality. By strict logic on the basis of modern discoveries that is not defensible, but is a self constructed faith.

My attention is drawn again to the trail. Something has changed. Then I realized that the overcast must have lightened up one barely noticeable amount. It should be easy going from here on. Besides, I must be getting reasonably near the lodge.

FOURTEEN

Just ahead about 50 feet it is evident that the trail turns to the left, and the bluff on my right curves around in front of me. There seems to be a dark area at the base of it where the trail turns. Coming closer now I can see that it looks like the mouth of a cave. The desk clerk had mentioned that there was a cave on this trail, and that if I needed a place of refuge in case of trouble it would be ideal, for the temperature in it never gets as low as freezing. As I recall he said it probably wouldn't be below 40 degrees F.

Now I can see the entrance to it distinctly as I come to the turn. It's just about thirty feet from the side of the trail, and not much above the elevation of the trail. It's too bad I don't have time to explore it, but I don't have any paper to roll into the form of a torch. And heaven knows what kind of animals are back in it now at night.

The entrance looks like it's about five to six feet high and about ten feet wide. The thing is conveniently located; it's rather thoughtful of nature to have provided such a place of refuge. In a world such as this a person needs that now and then, not so much from nature as from the world of people. After a fashion, the church, the Kingdom of God, provides that – a place of refuge from what is often the sin and grief of a world of people ruled by "the Prince of this world," as Jesus referred to him. At least for all practical purposes it seems to be ruled by him. The church, the outpost of the Kingdom of God, the City of God, through history and at its best, has proved to be a place of refuge for those who have been hurt and broken by sin — both their own and that done to them by other people. And it has been a refuge and a place of hope for those who counted themselves but pilgrims, and looked for the hope of life beyond this physical phase of existence. From the hatred and selfishness sometimes characteristic of people – for unregenerate mankind is basically self-seeking — there has been a place of refuge in the unconditional love that Jesus both taught and exemplified. In its life as a select community, a voluntary community that tries to follow the ethic of Jesus, the church has had a healing effect on people. But, it's time to move on, and the cave is already out of sight.

Now my attention is drawn to the turn that I am approaching. Under these circumstances, any change in my situation demands my full attention, for safety's sake. Besides that, there is the natural curiosity about the unknown.

FIFTEEN

As I come around a turn, the ravine that the trail lies in widens out into a glen about a hundred or more feet wide at the base, and since I'm at a lower elevation now the bluffs that constitute the sides of it seem to tower over me, almost enfolding me. This place has sort of a majestic quality to it; it's the kind of place where you tend to take off your shoes because it's holy ground — not a very practical impulse now here in the snow.

Walking slower now because of the beauty of this glen, I don't feel the need to get back to the lodge so soon. About a hundred feet into the glen I stop. "It's quiet here. Not a sound. There is no perceptible breeze, and so there is no creaking of the trees, flexing in their cold stiffened condition. Not a sound. It isn't often that you find a place like this that is totally quiet. It's really kind of awe inspiring."

With the sensory perception of sound vanished, the sole perception of reality is visual; the only touch perception coming through the combat boots. In a way the view seems a little unreal for there is no motion. No motion at all. That is a rare thing to experience — no perceptible sound, and no perceptible motion. It's like being totally surrounded by an artist's winter landscape, only in three dimensions. It seems like the longer I stand here the more majestically unreal and awe-inspiring it becomes — no sound, no motion, just visual, black on white, with the delicately intricate maze of tree branches and trunks in black against pure white. It is "the sound of one hand clapping." Much as I hate to break the enthrallment of this scene, I must move on. It seems like a desecration now, just to make the low sound of footsteps on snow. Nature here seems friendlier than any other place I've been. It's like walking through God's own winter cathedral. There's a friendliness to it that seems to communicate an invitation to come back when I have more time. But I must be going on now, and there is only another hundred and fifty feet to the exit of the glen. As I walk slowly along, looking around from time to time, the view changes slightly every twenty feet or so as I reach a new perspective of view of the bluffs. It's a strange situation to be confronted solely by the visual dimension of reality. Focusing on that one perception makes it come through in an intense manner. It is something that people rarely find, or make the opportunity to find. If they did perhaps it would be easier to put things in proper perspective — when reality confronts us in an overwhelming way it divests us of our petty concerns and produces a sobering effect.

SIXTEEN

In this situation I am currently in – not the valley of the shadow of death, but on the mountain of hope – there is a nearness to "the crack between the worlds." That perspective under-girds the prospect of the continuation of life beyond this earthly phase.

My memory takes me back to another time and place: Watching the hearse ahead turn into the cemetery at Valley Mills, Indiana is a sad thing, and not just because it is misting rain and the day is gloomy. Uncle Frank was a kind man — as kind as any I've known, if not more so. It seems a crying shame that his last years were so unhappy, spent in poverty. I guess in a way his kindness did that to him. As the cynical saying in Washington, D.C. goes, "No good deed goes unpunished." He could never refuse credit to anyone, and in the end his store was lost in bankruptcy.

He died in his sleep sitting in a chair. He had asked another uncle, who was living with him and his wife, to leave the door open a little. I guess the cool spring night air caused his asthma to kill him after he went to sleep.

The car turns slowly into the cemetery, and the driveway winds between the little hillocks and trees. There is a ground fog here and there between the hillocks, and the tombstones project through it as dismal reminders of our own mortality, "like tablets of the Law thrown down." Following the hearse now around a long turn to the left it comes to a stop just up ahead. After our car stops behind it my brothers and I, who are pallbearers, get out of the car and walk to the rear of the hearse. Slowly the casket slides out, and we hold it between us.

We have to turn left now and walk through about a hundred feet of ground fog to the hillock ahead with the awning over the grave. It seems unreal here; the fog swirls around our feet as we move through it. "What a lousy day for a funeral. But then, there never is a good day for a funeral. It's just that some are worse than others, and this is the worst I've seen." At last we arrive at the grave and slide the casket into place on the lowering device. Stepping back now, my mother and father and aunts and uncles take the seats reserved for the family.

The whole situation seems bizarre. The little hillock on which we stand is totally surrounded by the ground fog, and projects up out of it. Around about us at varying distances trees loom spookily up out of the fog and are dimly visible through the misting rain. Here and there other hillocks rise like islands out of a sea of fog. "This can't be happening."

Everybody is in place now and the minister begins,

I know that my Redeemer lives,
> and that in the end he will stand upon the earth.
And after my skin has been destroyed,
> yet in my flesh I will see God.
I myself will see him
> with my own eyes – I, and not another.

(Job 19:25-27)

Would to God that that will be true for Uncle Frank. May God rest his soul.

The minister drones on, "In sure and certain hope of the resurrection to eternal life through our Lord Jesus Christ, we commend to Almighty God our brother, and we commit his body to the ground, earth to earth, ashes to ashes, dust to dust. May he share in the fellowship and peace of all those in heaven with God now, until we meet again. Amen."

It is our only hope in the midst of this gloom and the desolation of death. It's times like this when it really hits home that the "good news" of the gospel is the promise of eternal life with God because of his love — because in his love he won't let the last word on a kind human life be six feet of earth in a gloomy, misty, country graveyard.

It is comforting also that the apostle Paul wrote to the Philippians, "I desire to depart and be with Christ, which is better by far." (1:23) He looked upon physical death as an immediate conscious entrance into the presence of Christ. In Hebrews 12, it states that those who are in heaven view the events of earth (probably just if they so choose). As it is, they surround us like a cloud of witnesses. From those passages, it is easy to dismiss such ideas as soul sleep or suspended animation.

When you add to that the fact that "time" as we know it, is a very this-worldly thing, a function of the ratio of mass and speed, and is interrelated with the three spatial dimensions. Once a person steps off of the continuum of time in the event of physical death, and into existence solely in the realm of the spirit, then time as we know it is probably irrelevant, except in watching the events of earth. But evidently there is in the realm of the spirit a form of time, a one-after-another-ness, a sequentiality of events, the context in which events happen. There is the statement in I John 3:2-3 that a Christian's existence in the realm of the spirit will be like Jesus', and therefore we can conclude: our personality will remain intact, we will be recognizable, and the limitations of time and space will no longer apply. We will be set free, with a far superior spiritual body no longer subject to the limitations of this material one – no longer subject to pain, decay, disease, aging, and death. Just as God refused to let sinful man's crucifixion of Jesus be the last word on his life which was lived by faith and unconditional love, and instead raised him to life in the spiritual dimension of existence, so also we, who follow after in faith and love, also have the promise of eternal life in the transcendence of the spirit. Therefore, there are better days ahead, and that enables us to lean into life and enjoy it. And as Ernest Hemingway stated: "This world is a fine place, and worth fighting for." This walk through a winter wonderland is proof of what Hemingway said. But I must keep moving on.

SEVENTEEN

Just ahead the glen narrows into a ravine again, and as I enter it there is a little regret at leaving the peace of the little valley behind. Here the ridge on my left and the bluff on my right slope sharply up about twenty feet from each side of the trail. About two hundred feet ahead the ridge curves across in front of me. Evidently the trail turns to the right there. That should put me back on about the right direction to the lodge.

There is a curious blend of a feeling of insignificance and significance here. The ridge and the bluff tower over me, and the darkness makes them seem all the more overwhelming. Yet at the same time, because I have seen no other animals it gives a strange sense of significance of being the only mobile living thing here. It gives almost a sense of supremacy to the stationary plant life.

The turn in the trail curves gradually to the right, and the mild slope to the land makes walking easy. It is always a curious thing to find out what is around each bend of the trail; it is a pleasant sense of expectancy without any threatening character to it for I feel at home here, even though I have never been here before.

Ahead the ravine widens out into another glen. It seems amazing that there would be two of them along this trail, almost in a row. As the ridge and bluff recede on each side there is a sense of expansiveness, and the trees in the little valley with the wooded steep slopes on each side make a beautiful scene. What a pity I don't have a camera with me with film sensitive enough to record the sight.

Being alone here gives the sensation of ownership — my own little valley, mine for a few minutes anyway. Awareness of a sound interrupts my thinking, and very faintly I can hear a gurgling sound of water flowing. After a few more feet a brook comes into view, flowing from the left side of the glen and turning to run parallel to the trail, just a half a dozen feet to the left of it. As I come closer to the place where it meets the trail it is interesting that the water looks black against the snow. I've read that in books before; I guess the authors must have spoken from first-hand experience.

Surely I have time to stop for a minute to watch and listen to the water flow. Kneeling down, in the soft snow at the edge of the brook, the water appears to be only gently troubled by the rocks over which it flows causing the sound. It must not be much more than half of a foot deep and only five or six feet wide. Listening to it now it almost seems like a companion and friend here beside me in this glen of mine. There is no other perceptible sound, other than that of the water which gives it a clear fullness to it, even though low in sound.

But it is time to go on, and it is pleasant to have such a companion for the journey. The thought is a little reminiscent of Jesus' words regarding living water — the water of life. If a person practices the presence of God, cultivates a sense of his presence, then I think that as the years go by there is an increasing openness to the dwelling of his Spirit within. But that varies from person to person.

It is interesting that in the Great Commission (Matthew 28:19) the Greek word that is often translated "in" would more accurately, and more in accord with its normal use, be translated "into." The corrected translation then is, "baptizing them into the name of," which indicates a spiritual union with God, an immersion into the very being of God. Such a translation is totally in accord with the New Testament concept of baptism. Presumably, as the years go by there is an increasing openness to that union, as the person's will more thoroughly and to a greater degree actively acknowledges the supremacy of God's will.

That gift of the Spirit of God within is our commonalty with God, our internal link. As such it can be a source of courage and consolation in the midst of the problems and troubles of life on this earth; however, it is better to use the word "challenges" (a positive oriented term), rather than problems and troubles (which are negatively oriented terms).

Our perception of God's presence is something that ideally grows as the years go by, as we open our life more and more to it, as we see events happen in our life that are just too good to attribute to "dumb luck," and yet are not in any way to be credited to our efforts.

We are called to be a part of the community of the family of God, as an adopted son or daughter of God. He chooses to call us into a personal relationship with him, even to the point of being a father to us, one who provides, protects, and cares for his own. And all the while, the beauty of nature, such as in this unspoiled glen, is a down payment on the fulfillment of our destiny as adopted sons and daughters of God.

EIGHTEEN

The glen proves to be only about three fourths of a mile long. Ahead, about a quarter of a mile it is evident that it narrows into a ravine again, but the sides are not as high there. The trail is a little steeper here, and it is evident that the valley slopes distinctly down. A birch tree stands particularly near the trail here on the right side of it and provides a hand hold over a slippery steep place.

As the ravine draws nearer I come to a rough wooden bridge over the brook which meanders to the right towards the bluff which is distinctly lower, only about eighty feet high. Farther on it is clear that it is sloping down to the level of the trail where it turns to meet it, and the ridge to my left also drops towards the level of the trail as it curves towards it. Both of them dish out to meet the trail, and in the far distance ahead I can see trees, but they look like they are nearly a mile away.

It looks like the trail dead ends up ahead on a bluff. As I come closer I can see and hear the brook cascading down the side of the mountain where the bluff on my right had been, but had flattened out and then sloped abruptly down as part of the mountain side. I seem to be approaching the edge of a cliff; as I come to about half a dozen feet from the edge it is evident that I am on a rocky cliff a hundred feet above the trail I started from.

Looking out to the south I can see a section of the forest covered mountain ridge in front of me. To the left, in a south-easterly direction is the river, and the dam forming a lake. The lake looks like it is about one thousand feet below where I now am. It also looks black against the snow. Turning to directly east, to my left, because the light draws my attention, I can see the lodge a hundred feet below and to the left, looking brilliantly lit up against the snow and the night sky. It looks garish there, like an alien intruder in the peaceable kingdom of this forest realm, in the tranquility of this winter night. The works of man look like a desecration here in the beauty of nature. From the perspective of the kingdom the actions of mankind in history have often seemed like that, and the redemptive activity of God through Christ initially, and through the church now, have been the only really mitigating factor.

The lodge looks like it is precariously perched there on a shelf of the mountain ridge. It represents the world of people, which sometimes includes desecration, and destruction of nature. There is an intense tendency now to turn around and go back into the forest. "Surely they wouldn't miss me if I stayed away a little longer. Perhaps I could hike just a little way along another trail, and enjoy, as much as time will allow me, the beauty of this night and of God's creation."

"But, No! They will be looking for me soon. I am fortunate that Maria has not yet sent somebody to search for me." I guess its time to go back, down into the world of people, a world much of which is alien to God and the tranquility I have known here.

The trail down the side of the cliff is steep and goes for a quarter of a mile. It's slippery and I have to carefully pick where I step. But time and distance seem to be passing quickly now.

As I reach the parapet of the lodge the light is so bright that it hurts my eyes. I turn to face the mountain that has surrendered me alive and well, as it would a friend. Looking at the mountain rising majestically in the night sky it seems a pity to leave it for the artificiality of the lodge, and it dawns on me that all during the journey I never uttered a prayer — but then, the journey itself was a prayer.

* * * * * * * * * *

REFERENCES of Interest

All references are from the New International Version of the Bible.

1. Genesis 3:1-24; 4:1-16
2. Isaiah 42:1-9
3. Matthew 28:16-20
4. Mark 10:13-16
5. John 10:35-39; Psalm 82:1-8
6. John 14:5-14
7. Acts 17:22-31
8. Romans 8:18-21
9. II Corinthians 5:11-6:2
10. Philippians 1:18-26
11. I Thessalonians 4:13-17
12. Ephesians 3:14-21

Also by Dr. Wm. Edwin Jacobs:

Answers to Unanswered Questions of Life and Religion
ISBN: 0-9778925-0-6

For information on, or to purchase copies of, the above book, please send the request to:

Victory Publishing Company
3797 North Ashley Court
Decatur, Illinois 62526-1291

Telephone # (217) 872–7401
e-mail: edmar84@aol.com

Please send the price of the book: $14.00
plus shipping expense of $ 2.00
Total of $16.00

Discounts are available for purchase of 5 or more.